PCOS COOKBOOK

40+Tart, Ice-Cream, and Pie recipes for a healthy and balanced PCOS diet

TABLE OF CONTENTS

Introduction

PCOS recipes for personal enjoyment but also for family enjoyment. You will love them for sure for how easy it is to prepare them.

BREAKFAST RECIPES

CHEESE AND GARLIC WEDGES

Serves: **4**

Prep Time: **10**   Minutes

Cook Time: **30**   Minutes

Total Time: **40**   Minutes

INGREDIENTS

- 3 pita bread
- ¼ lb. low-salt margarine
- 2 cloves garlic
- 2 tablespoons basil
- ½ cup parmesan cheese

DIRECTIONS

1. Preheat oven to 325 F
2. Split pita bread in half and cut into 4 wedges
3. Mix basil, garlic and margarine
4. Brush bread with mixture and sprinkle with parmesan cheese
5. Place in a single payer on oven and bake for 8-10 minutes or until crisp
6. Remove and serve

PARMESAN CRAKCKERS

Serves: **4**

Prep Time: **10** Minutes

Cook Time: **10** Minutes

Total Time: **20** Minutes

INGREDIENTS

- 6 tablespoons low-salt margarine
- 1 cup parmesan cheese
- 1 egg yolk
- ½ cup water
- 2 cups plain flour

DIRECTIONS

1. Preheat oven to 350 F
2. In a bowl mix flour with margarine, add egg yolk, cheese and mix well
3. Add water to the dough and divide dough into 2 portions
4. Cut into individual crackers and place on a baking sheet
5. Bake for 8-10 minutes or until brown, remove and serve

SESAME TWIST

Serves: **4**

Prep Time: **10**   Minutes

Cook Time: **30**   Minutes

Total Time: **40**   Minutes

INGREDIENTS

- 2 oz. low salt margarine
- 2 tablespoons sesame seeds
- 2 tablespoons parmesan cheese
- 2 tablespoons poppy seeds

DIRECTIONS

1. Preheat oven to 350 F
2. Cut pastry sheets in half and brush with butter
3. Mix cheese, sesame seeds and poppy
4. Sprinkle over pastry and cut into small strips
5. Place into greased baking trays and bake for 8-10 minutes or until golden brown
6. Remove and serve

OAT BISCUITS

Serves: **4**

Prep Time: **10**   Minutes

Cook Time: **30**   Minutes

Total Time: **40**   Minutes

INGREDIENTS

- ½ cup sugar
- 1/3 lb. low-salt margarine
- 1 tablespoon honey
- 1 cup flour
- 1 tsp baking powder
- ¼ tsp cinnamon
- 1 cup oats

DIRECTIONS

1. Preheat oven to 300 F
2. Cream margarine, honey and sugar, sift cinnamon, flour and baking powder
3. Add oats to the mixture and roll mixture into balls
4. Place on a greased oven tray and bake for 12-15 minutes or until golden brown, remove and serve

TOFU SCRAMBLE WITH POTATOES

Serves: **4**
Prep Time: **10**   Minutes

Cook Time: **15**   Minutes

Total Time: **25**   Minutes

INGREDIENTS
- 5 oz. tofu
- 1 cup mushrooms
- 1 cup onions
- 1 sweet potato
- 1 tablespoon coconut oil
- 1 cup spinach

DIRECTIONS

1. Wrap tofu in a towel and cover for a couple of minutes
2. Dice tofu and sweet potato
3. In a pan heat oil over medium heat and sauté tofu and potatoes
4. Add mushrooms, onions, spinach and sauté
5. Remove and serve

OVERNIGHT OATS

Serves: **2**
Prep Time: **10**   Minutes

Cook Time: **10**   Minutes

Total Time: **20**   Minutes

INGREDIENTS

- 1 tablespoon maple syrup
- 1 cup rolled oats
- 1 cup almond milk
- 1 tablespoon peanut butter
- 2 cup blueberries
- ¼ tablespoon cinnamon
- 1 banana
- 3 tablespoons chia seeds

DIRECTIONS

1. In a bowl mix all ingredients
2. Cover and refrigerate
3. Serve in the morning

AVOCADO TOAST

Serves: **2**
Prep Time: **10**   Minutes

Cook Time: **10**   Minutes

Total Time: **20**   Minutes

INGREDIENTS

- 1 slice bread
- 1 tablespoon lemon juice
- ½ tsp pepper
- ½ avocado
- ½ tablespoon chia seeds
- 1/3 tablespoons sunflower seed

DIRECTIONS

1. Mash the avocado and combine with sunflower seeds and chia seeds
2. Add lemon juice, pepper and mix well
3. Spread onto the toast and top with seeds

GOAT CHEESE AND PARSLEY SCRAMBLE

Serves: **2**

Prep Time: **10** Minutes

Cook Time: **10** Minutes

Total Time: **20** Minutes

INGREDIENTS

- 2 eggs
- ½ dash pepper
- 1 tsp olive oil
- ½ cup tomatoes
- 1 tablespoon parsley
- 1 oz. goat cheese
- 1 slice bread

DIRECTIONS

1. In a bowl whisk pepper and eggs
2. In a skillet heat oil and pour egg mixture and cook slowly
3. Add tomatoes and parsley and sprinkle with goat cheese
4. Cook for 1-2 minutes per side remove and serve

VANILLA PUDDING

Serves: **2**

Prep Time: **10**   Minutes

Cook Time: **10**   Minutes

Total Time: **20**   Minutes

INGREDIENTS

- 1 cup almond milk
- 1 tablespoon maple syrup
- 1 tablespoon vanilla extract
- ¼ tsp cinnamon
- ¼ tsp ginger
- ½ tsp cardamom
- ½ tsp cloves
- 2 tablespoons chia seed

DIRECTIONS

1. In a container add all ingredients and whisk together until well incorporated
2. Refrigerate overnight, remove and serve

BANANA PANCAKES

Serves: *1*

Prep Time: *10*   Minutes

Cook Time: *10*   Minutes

Total Time: *20*   Minutes

INGREDIENTS

- 1 egg
- 1 scoop protein powder
- 1 banana
- 1 stevia
- ½ tsp baking powder

DIRECTIONS

1. **In a bowl mix all ingredients, mix until every ingredient is incorporated**
2. **Pour mixture into a skillet and cook for 1-2 minutes per side**
3. **Remove and serve**

COCONUT QUINOA

Serves: **4**

Prep Time: **10**   Minutes

Cook Time: **30**   Minutes

Total Time: **40**   Minutes

INGREDIENTS

- 1 cup quinoa
- 1 cup coconut milk
- 1 cup pumpkin and squash seeds
- 1 cup water
- 1 cup strawberries

DIRECTIONS

1. In a pot add quinoa and coconut milk, stir in the rest of ingredients and boil
2. Lower the heat and simmer for 12-15 minutes
3. Add water if necessary
4. Divide into portions and top with berries

TOMATO SCRAMBLE

Serves: **4**

Prep Time: **10**   Minutes

Cook Time: **10**   Minutes

Total Time: **20**   Minutes

INGREDIENTS

- ½ tablespoon olive oil
- 2 tsp parsley
- 1 tsp pepper
- 1 slice bread
- 1 tomato
- 1 egg

DIRECTIONS

1. Chop tomato and fry with olive oil
2. Remove from pan and set aside
3. Scramble eggs, add tomatoes, parsley and pepper
4. Cook for 1-2 minutes per side, remove and serve

BREAKFAST BURRITO

Serves: **2**

Prep Time: **10** Minutes

Cook Time: **10** Minutes

Total Time: **20** Minutes

INGREDIENTS

- ½ cup brown rice
- 2 eggs
- 1 tablespoon salsa
- 1 tortilla
- 1 red bell pepper
- ½ avocado

DIRECTIONS

1. Chop bell pepper and avocado, set aside
2. In a bowl crack an egg and scramble, pour into a pan and cook on low heat
3. Combine egg with rice, bell pepper, salsa and avocado
4. Pour mixture into tortilla and serve

PINEAPPLE PUDDING

Serves: **2**

Prep Time: **10**   Minutes

Cook Time: **10**   Minutes

Total Time: **20**   Minutes

INGREDIENTS

- 1 cup almond milk
- 1 scoop protein powder
- ½ cup pineapple
- 1 tablespoon chia seeds

DIRECTIONS

1. In a container mix all ingredients
2. Refrigerate for at least one hour
3. Remove and serve

SRIRACHA BREAKFAST BOWL

Serves: **4**

Prep Time: **10** Minutes

Cook Time: **20** Minutes

Total Time: **30** Minutes

INGREDIENTS

- 1 cup rice
- 1 tsp soy sauce
- ¾ tsp sauce
- 6 tablespoons sesame oil
- ½ cup pineapple
- 1 stalk onion
- 1 egg
- 1 dash pepper

DIRECTIONS

1. Cook rice according directions
2. Season with sriracha, sesame oil and soy sauce
3. Chop pineapple and slice onion and stir in rice
4. Fry the egg and season and top the rice bowl with the egg and serve

BANANA PANCAKES

Serves: **4**

Prep Time: **10**   Minutes

Cook Time: **20**   Minutes

Total Time: **30**   Minutes

INGREDIENTS

- 1 cup whole wheat flour
- ¼ tsp baking soda
- ¼ tsp baking powder
- 1 cup banana
- 2 eggs
- 1 cup milk

DIRECTIONS

1. In a bowl combine all ingredients together and mix well
2. In a skillet heat olive oil
3. Pour ¼ of the batter and cook each pancake for 1-2 minutes per side
4. When ready remove from heat and serve

CRANBERRIES PANCAKES

Serves: **4**

Prep Time: **10**   Minutes

Cook Time: **30**   Minutes

Total Time: **40**   Minutes

INGREDIENTS

- 1 cup whole wheat flour
- ¼ tsp baking soda
- ¼ tsp baking powder
- 1 cup cranberries
- 2 eggs
- 1 cup milk

DIRECTIONS

1. In a bowl combine all ingredients together and mix well
2. In a skillet heat olive oil
3. Pour ¼ of the batter and cook each pancake for 1-2 minutes per side
4. When ready remove from heat and serve

DATE PANCAKES

Serves: **4**

Prep Time: **10** Minutes

Cook Time: **20** Minutes

Total Time: **30** Minutes

INGREDIENTS

- 1 cup whole wheat flour
- ¼ tsp baking soda
- ¼ tsp baking powder
- 1 tablespoons date fruit
- 2 eggs
- 1 cup milk

DIRECTIONS

1. In a bowl combine all ingredients together and mix well
2. In a skillet heat olive oil
3. Pour ¼ of the batter and cook each pancake for 1-2 minutes per side
4. When ready remove from heat and serve

PAPAYA MUFFINS

Serves: *8-12*
Prep Time: *10*   Minutes
Cook Time: *20*   Minutes
Total Time: *30*   Minutes

INGREDIENTS

- 2 eggs
- 1 tablespoon olive oil
- 1 cup milk
- 2 cups whole wheat flour
- 1 tsp baking soda
- ¼ tsp baking soda
- 1 tsp cinnamon
- 1 cup papaya

DIRECTIONS

1. In a bowl combine all dry ingredients
2. In another bowl combine all dry ingredients
3. Combine wet and dry ingredients together
4. Fold in papaya and mix well
5. Pour mixture into 8-12 prepared muffin cups, fill 2/3 of the cups
6. Bake for 18-20 minutes at 375 F

7. When ready remove from the oven and serve

PEAR MUFFINS

Serves: *8-12*
Prep Time: *10*   Minutes
Cook Time: *20*   Minutes
Total Time: *30*   Minutes

INGREDIENTS

- 2 eggs
- 1 tablespoon olive oil
- 1 cup milk
- 2 cups whole wheat flour
- 1 tsp baking soda
- ¼ tsp baking soda
- 1 tsp cinnamon
- 1 cup pear

DIRECTIONS

1. In a bowl combine all dry ingredients
2. In another bowl combine all dry ingredients
3. Combine wet and dry ingredients together
4. Fold in pear and mix well
5. Pour mixture into 8-12 prepared muffin cups, fill 2/3 of the cups
6. Bake for 18-20 minutes at 375 F

7. When ready remove from the oven and serve

CHOCOLATE MUFFINS

Serves: **8-12**

Prep Time: **10**   Minutes

Cook Time: **20**   Minutes

Total Time: **30**   Minutes

INGREDIENTS

- 2 eggs
- 1 tablespoon olive oil
- 1 cup milk
- 2 cups whole wheat flour
- 1 tsp baking soda
- ¼ tsp baking soda
- 1 tsp cinnamon
- 1 cup chocolate chips

DIRECTIONS

1. In a bowl combine all dry ingredients
2. In another bowl combine all dry ingredients
3. Combine wet and dry ingredients together
4. Fold in chocolate chips and mix well
5. Pour mixture into 8-12 prepared muffin cups, fill 2/3 of the cups
6. Bake for 18-20 minutes at 375 F

7. When ready remove from the oven and serve

PEACHES MUFFINS

Serves: **8-12**

Prep Time: **10**   Minutes

Cook Time: **20**   Minutes

Total Time: **30**   Minutes

INGREDIENTS

- 2 eggs
- 1 tablespoon olive oil
- 1 cup milk
- 2 cups whole wheat flour
- 1 tsp baking soda
- ¼ tsp baking soda
- 1 tsp cinnamon
- 1 cup peaches

DIRECTIONS

1. In a bowl combine all dry ingredients
2. In another bowl combine all dry ingredients
3. Combine wet and dry ingredients together
4. Pour mixture into 8-12 prepared muffin cups, fill 2/3 of the cups
5. Bake for 18-20 minutes at 375 F
6. When ready remove from the oven and serve

ASPARAGUS OMELETTE

Serves: *1*
Prep Time: *5*   Minutes

Cook Time: *10*   Minutes

Total Time: *15*   Minutes

INGREDIENTS

- 2 eggs
- ¼ tsp salt
- ¼ tsp black pepper
- 1 tablespoon olive oil
- ¼ cup cheese
- ¼ tsp basil
- 1 cup asparagus

DIRECTIONS

1. In a bowl combine all ingredients together and mix well
2. In a skillet heat olive oil and pour the egg mixture
3. Cook for 1-2 minutes per side
4. When ready remove omelette from the skillet and serve

ZUCCHINI OMELETTE

Serves: **1**

Prep Time: **5** Minutes

Cook Time: **10** Minutes

Total Time: **15** Minutes

INGREDIENTS

- 2 eggs
- ¼ tsp salt
- ¼ tsp black pepper
- 1 tablespoon olive oil
- ¼ cup cheese
- ¼ tsp basil
- 1 cup zucchini

DIRECTIONS

1. In a bowl combine all ingredients together and mix well
2. In a skillet heat olive oil and pour the egg mixture
3. Cook for 1-2 minutes per side
4. When ready remove omelette from the skillet and serve

BROCCOLI OMELETTE

Serves: *1*

Prep Time: *5*   Minutes

Cook Time: *10*   Minutes

Total Time: *15*   Minutes

INGREDIENTS

- 2 eggs
- ¼ tsp salt
- ¼ tsp black pepper
- 1 tablespoon olive oil
- ¼ cup cheese
- ¼ tsp basil
- 1 cup red onion
- 1 cup broccoli

DIRECTIONS

1. In a bowl combine all ingredients together and mix well
2. In a skillet heat olive oil and pour the egg mixture
3. Cook for 1-2 minutes per side
4. When ready remove omelette from the skillet and serve

BRUSSELS SPROUTS OMELETTE

Serves: **1**

Prep Time: **5**   Minutes

Cook Time: **10**   Minutes

Total Time: **15**   Minutes

INGREDIENTS

- 2 eggs
- ¼ tsp salt
- ¼ tsp black pepper
- 1 tablespoon olive oil
- ¼ cup cheese
- ¼ tsp basil
- 1 cup brussels sprouts

DIRECTIONS

1. In a bowl combine all ingredients together and mix well
2. In a skillet heat olive oil and pour the egg mixture
3. Cook for 1-2 minutes per side
4. When ready remove omelette from the skillet and serve

ARUGULA OMELETTE

Serves: *1*

Prep Time: *5*   Minutes

Cook Time: *10*   Minutes

Total Time: *15*   Minutes

INGREDIENTS

- 2 eggs
- ¼ tsp salt
- ¼ tsp black pepper
- 1 tablespoon olive oil
- ¼ cup cheese
- ¼ tsp basil
- 1 cup arugula

DIRECTIONS

1. In a bowl combine all ingredients together and mix well
2. In a skillet heat olive oil and pour the egg mixture
3. Cook for 1-2 minutes per side
4. When ready remove omelette from the skillet and serve

HAZELNUT TART

Serves: **6-8**

Prep Time: **25**   Minutes

Cook Time: **25**   Minutes

Total Time: **50**   Minutes

INGREDIENTS

- pastry sheets
- 3 oz. brown sugar
- ¼ lb. hazelnuts
- 100 ml double cream
- 2 tablespoons syrup
- ¼ lb. dark chocolate
- 2 oz. butter

DIRECTIONS

1. Preheat oven to 400 F, unfold pastry sheets and place them on a baking sheet
2. Toss together all ingredients together and mix well
3. Spread mixture in a single layer on the pastry sheets
4. Before baking decorate with your desired fruits
5. Bake at 400 F for 22-25 minutes or until golden brown

6. When ready remove from the oven and serve

PEAR TART

Serves: *6-8*
Prep Time: **25**   Minutes

Cook Time: **25**   Minutes

Total Time: *50*   Minutes

INGREDIENTS

- 1 lb. pears
- 2 oz. brown sugar
- ½ lb. flaked almonds
- ¼ lb. porridge oat
- 2 oz. flour
- ¼ lb. almonds
- pastry sheets
- 2 tablespoons syrup

DIRECTIONS

1. Preheat oven to 400 F, unfold pastry sheets and place them on a baking sheet
2. Toss together all ingredients together and mix well
3. Spread mixture in a single layer on the pastry sheets
4. Before baking decorate with your desired fruits
5. Bake at 400 F for 22-25 minutes or until golden brown
6. When ready remove from the oven and serve

PEACH PECAN PIE

Serves: **8-12**

Prep Time: **15**   Minutes

Cook Time: **35**   Minutes

Total Time: **50**   Minutes

INGREDIENTS

- **4-5 cups peaches**
- **1 tablespoon preserves**
- **1 cup sugar**
- **4 small egg yolks**
- **¼ cup flour**
- **1 tsp vanilla extract**

DIRECTIONS

1. Line a pie plate or pie form with pastry and cover the edges of the plate depending on your preference
2. In a bowl combine all pie ingredients together and mix well
3. Pour the mixture over the pastry
4. Bake at 400-425 F for 25-30 minutes or until golden brown
5. When ready remove from the oven and let it rest for 15 minutes

BUTTERFINGER PIE

Serves: **8-12**

Prep Time: **15** Minutes

Cook Time: **35** Minutes

Total Time: **50** Minutes

INGREDIENTS

- pastry sheets
- 1 package cream cheese
- 1 tsp vanilla extract
- ¼ cup peanut butter
- 1 cup powdered sugar (to decorate)
- 2 cups Butterfinger candy bars
- 8 oz whipped topping

DIRECTIONS

1. Line a pie plate or pie form with pastry and cover the edges of the plate depending on your preference
2. In a bowl combine all pie ingredients together and mix well
3. Pour the mixture over the pastry
4. Bake at 400-425 F for 25-30 minutes or until golden brown
5. When ready remove from the oven and let it rest for 15 minutes

STRAWBERRY PIE

Serves: **8-12**

Prep Time: **15** Minutes

Cook Time: **35** Minutes

Total Time: **50** Minutes

INGREDIENTS

- pastry sheets
- 1,5 lb. strawberries
- 1 cup powdered sugar
- 2 tablespoons cornstarch
- 1 tablespoon lime juice
- 1 tsp vanilla extract
- 2 eggs
- 2 tablespoons butter

DIRECTIONS

1. Line a pie plate or pie form with pastry and cover the edges of the plate depending on your preference
2. In a bowl combine all pie ingredients together and mix well
3. Pour the mixture over the pastry
4. Bake at 400-425 F for 25-30 minutes or until golden brown
5. When ready remove from the oven and let it rest for 15 minutes

BLUEBERRY PIE

Serves: *8-12*

Prep Time: *15*   Minutes

Cook Time: *35*   Minutes

Total Time: *50*   Minutes

INGREDIENTS

- pastry sheets
- ¼ tsp lavender
- 1 cup brown sugar
- 4-5 cups blueberries
- 1 tablespoon lemon juice
- 1 cup almonds
- 2 tablespoons butter

DIRECTIONS

1. Line a pie plate or pie form with pastry and cover the edges of the plate depending on your preference
2. In a bowl combine all pie ingredients together and mix well
3. Pour the mixture over the pastry
4. Bake at 400-425 F for 25-30 minutes or until golden brown
5. When ready remove from the oven and let it rest for 15 minutes

PEANUT BUTTER SMOOTHIE

Serves: *1*

Prep Time: *5*   Minutes

Cook Time: *5*   Minutes

Total Time: *10* Minutes

INGREDIENTS

- 1 cup soy milk
- 1 banana
- 1 tablespoon peanut butter
- ¼ tsp cinnamon
- 1 cup ice

DIRECTIONS

1. In a blender place all ingredients and blend until smooth
2. Pour smoothie in a glass and serve

SPINACH SMOOTHIE

Serves: **1**

Prep Time: **5** Minutes

Cook Time: **5** Minutes

Total Time: **10** Minutes

INGREDIENTS

- 1 banana
- 1 cup ice
- ¼ cup blueberries
- 1 cup spinach

DIRECTIONS

1. In a blender place all ingredients and blend until smooth
2. Pour smoothie in a glass and serve

STRAWBERRY SMOOTHIE

Serves: **1**

Prep Time: **5**   Minutes

Cook Time: **5**   Minutes

Total Time: **10** Minutes

INGREDIENTS

- 1 cup strawberries
- 1 cup cranberry juice
- ½ cup orange juice
- 1 cup vanilla yogurt

DIRECTIONS

1. In a blender place all ingredients and blend until smooth
2. Pour smoothie in a glass and serve

VEGAN CHOCOLATE SMOOTHIE

Serves: **1**

Prep Time: **5**   Minutes

Cook Time: **5**   Minutes

Total Time: **10** Minutes

INGREDIENTS

- 2 bananas
- 2 tablespoons cocoa powder
- 1 tablespoon maple syrup
- ½ cup peanut butter
- 1 cup ice
- 2 cups almond milk

DIRECTIONS

1. In a blender place all ingredients and blend until smooth
2. Pour smoothie in a glass and serve

AVOCADO SMOOTHIE

Serves: *1*

Prep Time: 5   Minutes

Cook Time: 5   Minutes

Total Time: *10*   Minutes

INGREDIENTS

- 1 avocado
- 2 cups mango juice
- 1 cup orange juice
- 1 cup ice

DIRECTIONS

1. In a blender place all ingredients and blend until smooth
2. Pour smoothie in a glass and serve

Serves: **1**

Prep Time: **5** Minutes

Cook Time: **5** Minutes

Total Time: **10** Minutes

INGREDIENTS

- 1 cup tomato juice
- ½ cup carrot juice
- 1 celery
- 1 cup spinach
- 1 cucumber
- 1 cup ice

DIRECTIONS

1. In a blender place all ingredients and blend until smooth
2. Pour smoothie in a glass and serve

ICE-CREAM RECIPES

PISTACHIOS ICE-CREAM

Serves: **6-8**

Prep Time: **15**   Minutes

Cook Time: **15**   Minutes

Total Time: **30**   Minutes

INGREDIENTS

- 4 egg yolks
- 1 cup heavy cream
- 1 cup milk
- 1 cup sugar
- 1 vanilla bean
- 1 tsp almond extract
- 1 cup cherries
- ½ cup pistachios

DIRECTIONS

1. In a saucepan whisk together all ingredients
2. Mix until bubbly
3. Strain into a bowl and cool
4. Whisk in favorite fruits and mix well
5. Cover and refrigerate for 2-3 hours

6. Pour mixture in the ice-cream maker and follow manufacturer instructions

7. Serve when ready

VANILLA ICE-CREAM

Serves: **6-8**

Prep Time: **15**   Minutes

Cook Time: **15**   Minutes

Total Time: **30**   Minutes

INGREDIENTS

- 1 cup milk
- 1 tablespoon cornstarch
- 1 oz. cream cheese
- 1 cup heavy cream
- 1 cup brown sugar
- 1 tablespoon corn syrup
- 1 vanilla bean

DIRECTIONS

1. In a saucepan whisk together all ingredients
2. Mix until bubbly
3. Strain into a bowl and cool
4. Whisk in favorite fruits and mix well
5. Cover and refrigerate for 2-3 hours
6. Pour mixture in the ice-cream maker and follow manufacturer instructions
7. Serve when ready

THANK YOU FOR READING THIS BOOK!

CPSIA information can be obtained
at www.ICGtesting.com
Printed in the USA
LVHW021318270321
682676LV00001B/79

9 781664 057661